START-UP
CITIZENSHIP

ANIMALS AND US

Louise and Richard Spilsbury

Evans

Published by Evans Brothers Limited
2A Portman Mansions
Chiltern Street
London W1U 6NR

© Evans Brothers Limited 2007

Produced for Evans Brothers Limited by
White-Thomson Publishing Ltd.
Bridgewater Business Centre, 210 High Street,
Lewes, East Sussex BN7 2NH

Printed in China by WKT Co. Ltd.

Editor: Clare Collinson
Consultant: Roy Honeybone, Consultant in Citizenship
Education and Editor of *Teaching Citizenship*, the
journal of the Association for Citizenship Teaching
Designer: Leishman Design

British Library Cataloguing in Publication Data
Spilsbury, Louise
    Animals and us - (Start-up citizenship)
    1. Animal welfare - Juvenile literature
    2. Human-animal relationships - Juvenile literature
    3. Citizenship - Juvenile literature
    I. Title II. Spilsbury, Richard, 1963-
    179.3

ISBN-13: 978 0 237 53264 2

Acknowledgements:
Special thanks to the following for their help and
involvement in the preparation of this book: staff, pupils
and parents at St Stephen's CE First School, Redditch;
Dudley's Coaches, Inkeberrow.

Picture Acknowledgements:
Alamy/Wildscape p. 8; The Blue Cross 17t; Martyn
Chillmaid p. 14r; Corbis pp. 10, 15 (Federico
Gambarini/dpa); Drusillas Park, East Sussex p. 14l;
iStockphoto.com pp. 4, 6l, 9 (both); RSPCA pp. 5b
(Susan and Allan Parker), 6r (Jonathan Plant), title page
and 7l (Angela Hampton), 11t (Andrew Linscott), 11b
(Angela Hampton), 12l (Angela Hampton), 12r (Angela
Hampton), 16t (Colin Seddon), 16b (Andrew Forsyth),
17b (Andrew Forsyth), 18 (both) (Andrew Forsyth),
19 (both) (Andrew Forsyth), 20 (Andrew Forsyth),
21l (Paul Herrmann); WTPix cover, pp. 5t (Robert
Pickett), 13.

Artwork:
Hattie Spilsbury pp. 7, 21.

Contents

Thinking about animals

What do animals need to be healthy and happy?
How do wild animals, farm animals and pets get
the things they need?

need   healthy   wild   pets

► A guinea pig needs to be given fresh water and hay every day. How are a pet's needs **similar** to ours? How are they **different**?

► There are **laws** to **protect** animals and their needs. It is against the law to harm a bird, its nest or its eggs.

similar   different   laws   protect

Animal habitats

The place where an animal lives is called its habitat. Gardens, ponds and woods are types of animal habitat.

▲ Many squirrels live in woodland habitats. They eat nuts from the trees.

▲ People can spoil animal habitats by dropping litter. Animals may choke on plastic or get stuck inside bottles and cans.

habitat   woodland   litter

▲ The Countryside Code is a set of **rules** for people who visit the countryside. One of the rules asks people to keep their dogs on leads in places where they could scare farm animals or **wildlife**.

WHEN VISITING WILD PLACES :

Keep to the paths.

Close gates behind you.

Take your litter home.

Don't damage or remove flowers/plants.

Leave animals alone

▲ What rules would you make to protect animals and their habitats?

rules   wildlife

Minibeasts

Minibeasts are invertebrates. These are animals such as spiders, worms and insects that do not have bones inside. Many are small and live in habitats such as gardens and ponds.

We have a responsibility to protect all animals. When you study invertebrates try not to handle or scare them.

invertebrates   insects   responsibility

Minibeasts are useful. They recycle waste, for example by eating dead leaves.

▶ We can help minibeasts in our gardens by leaving flowerpots or piles of logs for them to shelter in.

◀ Some insects live and work together. Some of these ants have made a bridge so that others can carry food across and take it back to the nest. How can people learn from this behaviour?

recycle   behaviour

Farm animals

Have you ever visited a farm? Sam and his family own a farm. They raise animals to provide people with eggs, meat and milk.

"In spring I feed some of the newborn lambs milk from a bottle."

Farmers are responsible for the welfare of their animals. They make sure the animals have everything they need.

raise   provide   welfare

► When a farm animal is sick the farmer pays a vet to come and make it better.

▼ The chickens on this farm roam in wide open spaces during the day. At night they go into a chicken house to be safe from foxes.

sick   vet   roam

Caring for pets

Which animal would you like to have as a pet?

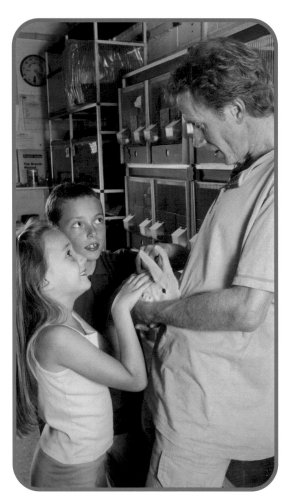

◄ When you choose a pet your family must be able to look after it properly and keep it safe, healthy and clean.

"I chose a hamster because they don't need a lot of space."

Why do you think people living in a small house or flat should not have a large dog as a pet?

properly   clean

It can be expensive to keep pets. Many pets need a cage or hutch, bedding and toys as well as food. They also need a check-up at the vet's every year and if they get ill.

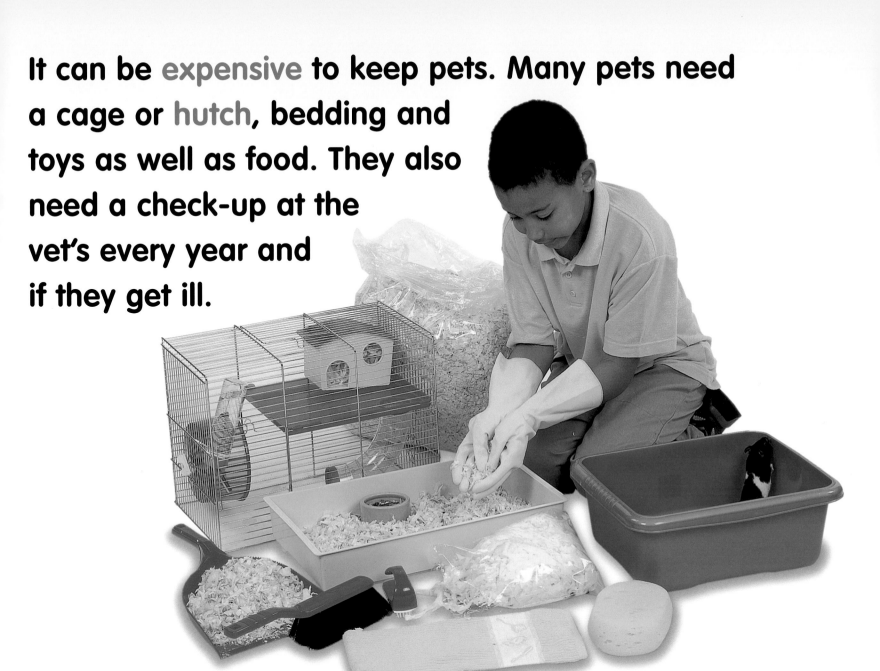

Pets need a lot of time and attention. You may need to walk or play with them every day. You should clean a pet hutch at least once a week.

expensive   hutch   attention

Going to the zoo

▶ Max's class help their teacher organise a trip to a zoo. Together they travel to the zoo by bus.

◀ At the zoo, the zookeeper explains that different animals need different kinds of food. Max helps the zookeeper feed fish to the penguins.

organise   zookeeper

Some people do not like zoos because animals are kept in cages. Other people say zoos help endangered animals. What do you think?

◄ This baby monkey's mother has died. The zookeeper is feeding it milk to help it survive.

Max's class do a survey to find out what people in the school think about zoos. Why is it important to find out what other people think?

endangered   survive   survey

Who helps animals?

There are many organisations that help animals.

▶ This fox injured its leg. The RSPCA treated it. Now the fox is being set free again.

◀ Rescue centres look after unwanted pets and pets that have been badly treated. They try to find new homes for them. How do you feel about people who do not look after their pets properly?

organisations   injured   unwanted

► **Some organisations use posters and leaflets to teach people about the problems animals face. What is this poster telling us?**

Many of the groups that help animals are charities. The work they do is paid for by donations. People give them money or raise funds at events like jumble sales.

A day in the life of an RSPCA officer

I am an RSPCA inspector. The letters RSPCA stand for Royal Society for the Prevention of Cruelty to Animals. I always wanted a job that involves looking after animals.

Checking a dog

10am. One of my jobs today is to check on a dog. A neighbour called to say the owner may not be caring for it properly. The animal is weak. I explain to the owner that it needs exercise. I'll come back in two weeks to check on the dog.

inspector   cruelty   exercise

Picking up a stray cat

2pm. After lunch, I pick up a stray cat that was almost run over. It does not have a collar with its name and address on, so I shall take it back to the RSPCA centre. Then we shall have to find it a new home.

4pm. In my car I get a call about a neglected parrot that I have seen before. This time I will have to remove the bird from the owner. I shall take it to the vet on my way home. I am looking forward to my tea and to taking my own dog for a run!

A call about a parrot

stray   neglected

Taking action

We can all help animals. Volunteers are people who give some time to help others.

▲ Some volunteers walk dogs for owners who are too old or ill to walk the animals themselves.

Why do you think people become volunteers? What could you do to help animals?

volunteers

◀ Jasmine's school is helping to protect a local stream habitat. First they spend a day clearing litter from the stream.

West marsh primary school marshland, England, BQ2 ZWD
12th december 2006.

Dear mr smith,

We are writing to ask you to save our stream. We have cleared the litter from the stream. Can the council put some rubbish bins nearby to stop people dropping litter? Can you put up a fence to stop dogs scaring the birds and other animals there.

Thank you for your help.

From class two.

▶ Then they write a letter to the council. They ask the council to protect the habitat and the animals that live there. Has your school helped a local animal habitat?

council

Further information for

New words listed in the text:

attention	endangered	insects	organise	roam	vet
behaviour	exercise	inspector	pets	rules	volunteers
charities	expensive	invertebrates	properly	sick	welfare
clean	funds	laws	protect	similar	wild
council	habitat	litter	provide	stray	wildlife
cruelty	healthy	need	raise	survey	woodland
different	hutch	neglected	recycle	survive	zookeeper
donations	injured	organisations	responsibility	unwanted	

Possible Activities

PAGES 4-5

Compare the basic needs of animals with the needs of people. Then discuss the difference between what we want and what we need. Discuss the needs of a particular animal, using soft toy animals as examples. Or pass around a puppet animal and ask children to say what it needs to be happy and healthy. Think about wild, pet and farm animals in these discussions.

PAGES 6-7

Ask children to think about their own habitats (such as their home or town) to help them understand that habitats can be big or small. Then explore the ways in which habitats differ, perhaps by observing habitats in the school grounds or local wild area. Discuss how animals are adapted, or suited, to the different habitats in which they live. Explore other ways in which people affect habitats, including taking over land for buildings or new roads, hedgerow cutting, road traffic, and the use of insecticides and pesticides.

PAGES 8-9

As a drama activity, ask the children to move as if they were an invertebrate. For example, they could walk sideways like a crab, slither along like a snail, scurry like a spider or wiggle like a worm. They could extend this by adding sounds, using instruments or found objects, to help them illustrate the different invertebrate movements. To encourage empathy, ask them how it feels to be in someone else's shoes (or shell). Linking with a science topic, ask children to think about the vital role invertebrates play in the food chain.

PAGES 10-11

You can download the RSPCA's 'The five freedoms' photocopiable factsheet at http://www.rspca.com. This explains the RSPCA's welfare standards for the care of farm and other animals. At http://www.farmtrails.org.uk you can visit real farms around the country and follow links that explain what they do and how they care for their animals.

Parents and Teachers

PAGES 12-13

At http://www.rspca.org.uk there is a children's maths activity called 'Thinking numbers' which gives figures for the different costs for keeping a dog for a year so the children can work out the total cost. Or children could work out a similar activity for another pet, by calculating how many bags of rabbit food a rabbit might need each year. This could link with a Growing up topic, where children think about the way an animal's needs change as it grows. Explain that the legal age for pet ownership is 12 and children must take an adult with them when choosing a pet. The children could discuss why this law exists. Do they agree with it?

PAGES 14-15

If planning a trip to the zoo, or other venue, children could be involved in thinking about some of the financial considerations. They could be given choices based on cost. Children could research and then design menus for different zoo animals such as monkeys and elephants to reinforce the idea that different animals need different kinds of food. Children could pretend they own their own zoo and plan what animals they would have there. What kind of enclosures would the different kinds of animals need?

PAGES 16-17

At http://www.uknetguide.co.uk/Lifestyle_and_Leisure/Pets/Animal_Charities.html there are links to 40 different animal charities and details about their different activities, including The Blue Cross, Britain's pet charity. Using the Animals Charities website pupils could research and then devise their own poster campaign for one of the organisations.

Further Information

BOOKS FOR CHILDREN

Animals Like Us (Dorling Kindersley, 2005)

Animals and Us (*Oxford Reading Tree series*) by Claire Llewellyn (Oxford University Press, 2005)

Animals and Us: Do Animals Have Rights? (*Get Wise series*) by Jane Bingham (Heinemann Library, 2005)

WEBSITES

http://www.rspca.org.uk

http://www.rspb.org.uk

http://www.farmtrails.org.uk

http://www.wwflearning.co.uk

PAGES 18-19

Children could learn about why and when the RSPCA was founded and how people's attitudes to animal cruelty have changed over the years. For information see http://www.rspca.co.uk and go to the link 'About the RSPCA'.

PAGES 20-21

Children could design a wildlife garden, or draw a plan of one, labelling features that help provide wild animals with what they need to live, such as a compost patch for invertebrates and bird feeder for garden birds.

Index